Quill of Written Voices

Nery Joy Ochea

Ukiyoto Publishing

All global publishing rights are held by

Ukiyoto Publishing

Published in 2023

Content Copyright © Nery Joy Ocheaa

ISBN 9789360160760

All rights reserved.
No part of this publication may be reproduced, transmitted, or stored in a retrieval system, in any form by any means, electronic, mechanical, photocopying, recording or otherwise, without the prior permission of the publisher.

The moral rights of the author have been asserted.

This is a work of fiction. Names, characters, businesses, places, events, locales, and incidents are either the products of the author's imagination or used in a fictitious manner. Any resemblance to actual persons, living or dead, or actual events is purely coincidental.

This book is sold subject to the condition that it shall not by way of trade or otherwise, be lent, resold, hired out or otherwise circulated, without the publisher's prior consent, in any form of binding or cover other than that in which it is published.

www.ukiyoto.com

Acknowledgements

I would love to dedicate this poem to my family, including my mother in heaven, my internet friends, my best friends, and, of course, to my special someone. Also, this is for everyone who believed in me that I would come to this point—I would be able to achieve my dream.

I thank God for giving me this opportunity to have my masterpieces finally come into print. He heard my prayers and the wishes of my heart.

SYNOPSIS

The Quill of Written Voices is written by Nery Joy Ochea, which weaves collection of poems, crafted by the author to explore and dive in human emotions and intricacies of life.

Through her heartfelt verses, Nery Joy aims to capture the raw essence of emotions, inviting readers to embark on a profound journey through the words of life.

As the readers flip every pages, they will find themselves deep in the ocean of a rich tapestry of emotions. The author fearlessly delves into the complexities of love, loss, joy, pain, and everything in between, painting vivid portraits of everybody's life experience. Each poem serves as a window into the depths of the soul, offering solace, understanding, and a profound sense of connection to those who have experienced similar emotions and situations. With a delicate touch, the author skillfully crafts verses that resonate with readers from all walks of life. These poems are a reflection of the universal human experience, capturing the essence of shared emotions and the intricacies of personal journeys. Through her words, the author invites readers to find solace in their own experiences, to embrace the beauty of vulnerability, and to discover the strength within themselves.

As readers delve deeper into the pages of the Quill of Written Voices, they will be inspired to continue fighting, living, and dreaming. Nery Joy's words serve as a gentle reminder that life is a tapestry of highs and lows, and that even in the darkest moments, there is always hope. Through evocative imagery and poignant metaphors, she encourages readers to embrace their own stories, find courage in their vulnerabilities, and seek the light even in the midst of darkness.

The poems in this collection are a testament to the power of words and their ability to touch the deepest corners of the every individual's heart. With each turn of the page, readers will find themselves captivated by the author's ability to paint emotions with her pen, to breathe life into words, and to create a symphony of emotions that reverberate within the soul.

The Quill of Written Voices is not simply a collection of poems; it is a heartfelt invitation to embrace the full spectrum of emotions that make everyone feel themselves. It serves as a reminder that life is a beautiful, messy, and extraordinary journey, and that through the power of words, everyone can find solace, inspiration, and the strength to continue fighting, living, and dreaming.

In the end, readers will close the book with a renewed sense of appreciation for the complexities of life, a deeper understanding of their own emotions, and a profound connection to the shared experience of every individual.

The Quill of Written Voices is a testament to the power of poetry to touch hearts, ignite souls, and inspire us to embrace the beauty and challenges of being alive. With every page turned, readers will be captivated by the author's ability to evoke emotions, provoke introspection, and leave an indelible mark on their hearts and minds.

Contents

The Blind's Favorite Color	1
Song of Our Touch	3
Soul for Sale	6
Penumbra	8
Aubergine Flower	9
War of Hope	12
Bring Me	14
The Naughty Crow	16
Symphony of the Sundered Hearts	18
Tagay, Waraynun: Beckon of Camaraderie	29
Goodnight Kiss in the Lionheart Street	30
Melancholy	33
Song of the Blues	34
Lullaby of One's Freedom	35
Chimeric tomorrow	37
Art of Society	39
Impostor	40
Art of Words	41
Withered Love	42
Azaleas	43
Morning Soul	44
Butterfly of Her Promise	45
Desire	47
Despair	49
Word of Advice	50
Painless Color	51
Fighters of the Forest	52
Fear Within	53

Shadow of Reality	54
Forgive for Freedom	56
Farewell Letter	57
Wish of the Hopeless Heart	58
Do You Remember You?	60
Hopelessly Hoping Ocean	63
Strong	64
Painfully Sweet Illusions	65
Thread of Life	66
Echoes of Lost Hope	67
Lost in the Whispers	68
Resonation of Absences	70
The Light Within	71
I Understand What I don't Understand	72
About the Author	*73*

The Blind's Favorite Color

I always wonder what the world looks like,
What might be the difference between sunset and sunrise?
I want to see the beautiful morning and cold night,
Under the so called sky that has stars that shine bright.

What it means to be pretty?
I always hear that from everybody.
They call me 'beautiful' or 'lovely'
I also hear some would say, "You're ugly."
Is it of the same meaning, I wonder?
I hope I have eyes that could see through a mirror.

Some would ask me about my favorite color,
Is it red, yellow, blue or purple?
I might be blind but I know the answer—
It's brown and no other.

Brown consists of two colors of life—
Euphoria and woe.
The color seen by our hearts are ignored all the time,
Most do not even realize it or simply do not know.
The shade of light represents the drum of laughter and great joy within;
Tinge of darkness brings the symbol of pain.

My favorite color screams the meaning of 'to live',

We should always look forward about what we can achieve.
We might cry, we might get hurt, we might fail,
But giving up is not always the option—in ourselves, we should believe!

My favorite color may represent somber to many,
But as how my mother tell me the meaning of 'beauty',
I could tell that brown is not about ageing and agony—
This color has hidden purity and sincerity.

If you come to the world of despondency,
Paint the brown color in your head.
Shade emptiness with the answer of why you are alive,
Rushing darkness within you—do not be afraid.
Warm your heart with the embrace of endless battle—
Battle of inspiration,
Let your peaceful heart bring forth your ambition.

Song of Our Touch

Fluffy cottons walking on the blue ceiling,
Cried upon the mourning grass.
Colorful lines painted across the bright colors,
Faded in a blink of an eye.
Yesterday, regrets and hopelessness walked on the isle of my life,
Kissed me the beauty of darkness—I embraced it.

My name is Kifa,
The child who was born with a dull destiny.
My mother left me in the hands of the soil,
Who took care of me until I was old.
I learned to dance with the wind of yesterday,
And sang with the lullabies of the present.
The morrow shall teach me how to live a life in the battle of hell,
My journey burns with sorrow and agony.

I do not know the name of the woman who birthed me,
Nor I have no knowledge about my family.
All I can remember is the beauty—
Beauty of nature, which saved me.
The warm grass held my hand;
Brought love to my cold heart.
Trees bowed on my face,
Carried me to the world of wonders.
Melody escaped my throat,

Birds sang lullabies with my chant of hope.

Several times, I had encountered,
A vague appearance of somebody.
A gorgeous string of hair swayed in the light of the rainbow,
Pretty thin lips awaken my heart.
A soft, melodious voice in my ears whispers,
Love that I never met in the real world.

Scintilla of touch crawls in my soul,
Yet I doubt what it means.
Her voice speaks fuzzy hues of our connection,
Breaking the design of trust.
Mother—they say, she is,
Yet it's hard to bring trust forward.
Dubiety wakes in my head,
Floating on the surface of a hungry and empty childhood.

One day, my feet walked on the smooth river,
Humming on the surface of absences—my mouth did.
Then, my ears tingled at the response from afar,
Coming from inside the dark forest—who could it be?
Frightened, yet I'm not,
Brought forward the armor of the ages,
Putting oneself in danger,
Whoever comes to put my death on the edge,
I shall come and prepare my soul on the ridge, I say.

The melodious voice kept responding to my hum,
Until it began to follow where I am.
My heart pondered—no, I'm not afraid,
Something wakes in me that brings me forward to hope—
Mother, the word in my head echoed.
I'm not ready—alas! Hide me away!

A gorgeous woman appeared before the sky,
String of her hair once again danced in the rainbow.
We both hum the lullaby of vague love—
She was the one who wrote it for me when I was a child.
Mother; she never left.
It was me who was lost in the meantime.

Soul for Sale

Fire of doubt swarmed unto my head,
I closed my eyes—saw the eagle of hatred.
Hands on the rails of death,
Touched the hues of hell on the ground.
Woke from another world—
Had a life of a reincarnated ferocity.
I called the name of heavens,
Yet blocked on the mouth of indignant kismet.

Kissed with the appellation of Light of Darkness;
Woe—it was a mistake, I say.
Drawn in the etiquette of doom,
Inside emptiness, I cry without tears alone.

I question the existence of anxiety and depression,
My wings flew away in despair,
Ember of sunlight fighting poignant,
Drew its last breath, apologizing to me.
I tried to run to save it,
Yet it was quite too late to bring the ones who disappeared.

Painted my own fate on a placard—
I AM FOR SALE, I wrote.
I stood alone by the emptiness,
Waiting for someone to pass and buy my life.

Scared I am—doubtful, yes,
Yet I'm tired of waiting for what's next.
Stepped on the soft road of wisdom,
Broke the bridge of a brighter light ahead.

Forgive me, for I have no reason to keep my life in the world,
Death beckons the paradise of loneliness—
My life, yes it is.
Sword of last breath passed by,
Why ignored the pleasure drooling on the wood in my chest?
Am I still invisible in the eyes of comeuppance?
Pleaded with my knees bleeding on the river of thorns,
Kneeled until torment killed my breath.

Penumbra

When sunlight caresses the doom,
Appears behind me the greatest person I know.
She does not know how to talk,
Yet she knows how to listen.
She memorizes everything I do,
She never failed to impersonate every move I make.

She might be born mute,
But I admire how we laugh together under the sunlight.
She never came forward as we walk together on the highway,
She always wants to by my side or behind.
I do not know her name,
Yet I call her Penumbra.

Aubergine Flower

Crackled paint swarmed on the walls,
Spiders designed the corners with their webs.
Leaves fallen off the plants on the window,
Painting on the canvas stayed on its stand behind the door.
Unfixed bed stayed in its place for weeks.

A woman in her wheelchair sits before the glass window,
Pours in her eyes sympathy on herself.
Shivering hands on her weak legs,
Became the strength for holding on to the remaining days.
Smile with millions of words to tell,
Disappeared with pale passion.

"Only the aubergine flower can bring back the smile of one's withered heart,
Yet it will be the symbol of last breath."
Happiness flows in her tone of melancholy,
Tint of great joy shines in her eyes.
"Love speaks in its motionless time,
Beneath the hours of a long run lies one's heart—not desires."

Smell of her wisdom lurked unto the tip of my nose,
However, my tongue escaped—
Altering the taste of her shade is strenuous.
Aubergine flower, the symbol of her death?

Why a beautiful creation became the angel of morbidity?
Perhaps something behind the closed door lies the answer,
I shall seek for it; the key borrows hidden debt on one's personage.

"Dear, the peak of your dreams is as far as the stars—
It's hard to climb the stairs without holding back.
Stepping away and away and away, you would,
However, do you think that it is the right path towards your wish?"
I understood no words from her mouth,
Her vision whispered blues of the night.
Wrote them blindfolded on a red note—
Deep-seated in the midst of darkness, lights the aubergine flower.

Days went by, the wheelchair became empty,
A leaf from a tree flew down on it,
Kissed the scent of her favorite perfume—sandalwood.
Zephyr visited, shoved the leaf away,
Came after a blue butterfly,
Pressed its small legs on the glass window, stared at me.
I waved hi—it flapped its wings away as if telling me thank you.

The aubergine flower from the window,
Seated bowing its head on the ground—dying.
Bitter smile curved in my lips,
Longing for her sweet smile every morning—Grandma.
One night, a dream bolted me awoke,
An aubergine flower held in her hand—

She was smiling at me.

She's walking on an endless void,

The flower lit up, showing her the way forward.

Now, I understood why she waited for the flower to bloom and die—

It's her guardian angel in the afterlife.

War of Hope

Hope-filled skies were obscured by the fire of the heavens,
Raining on the abandoned land
—the bullets from yesterday's fantasy.
Calling back the name of the soldier with a broken heart—
Broken by the crow's cry of sorrow.

Defenders of the unclad child-bearer,
The great impotence's alliance.
Bringing to the world of forgiveness—
Something which the raven of the night once devoured: hope.

Tomorrow the fire of the heavens will blow the wind of sorrow once again,
Alas! The soldiers will show up to support the battle of futility.
The valley of smiles dwindled—
Those who were unappeasable to him died at their hands.
Forgive, forgive, for they are deaf to the grave blunder.

Horns blowing to the west—
Alas! The beauty of hearts was deceived by fate.
Call forth the cries of the opposition,
Bring the flags with bullets of pride.
Keep one's hands on the incline of untimely doom,
Within the future's bark beats a fiery core.

Lullaby of the Forgotten Song

Torn apart was the string of hearts,
Down the route of arcs, memories were bleeding.
Weeping, she does,
Yet no tears of deception.
The doomed sky thundered beneath the great marks of loneliness,
Behold, the wind's hue blew at daybreak toward the south.

Humming alone by the shore,
The torrents of blazing wrath rolled in.
Continued humming—she did,
Calling the one who had forgotten her existence.

Sparkling eyes in the west,
Became the light of the dying coal of life.
Breath in every stream,
obstructed the nefarious leaf whispers.
In the orange sky, dispersed,
Silhouette of anguish and the raging torment of desires.

Bring Me

Through emptiness, the owls' cries could be heard.
Dark clouds streaming down into the pristine waters—
Ah, loneliness—that's what it is!
Bring me, bring me
My true love, who with his final breath showed mercy.
Broken vases of promises, I shall find every piece.

Bring me the color pencil of yesterday,
I shall use it to color the canvas of dread.
Alas! I have no remorse about the numerous tears that flowed throughout the space.
Hold my tongue,
Embrace the angel of the lonely heart.
Weep, weep, weep,
Until tears dry in my face.

My, my! The route taken by the dejected,
Confined space that is teeming with monsters—Oh my, I'm terrified!
Where can one find the wings of light that will lead to a better smile?
Oh, I humbly plead for it.
Bring me the person whose life I desire to own.
In this doomsday voyage, he is the light.

The ocean's deep-water eagle,
Soared above the million obstacles of life,

Oh, bring me that eagle that could take me far away from where I am.
Dying at the ravenous creatures' hands,
To be swallowed—I am insufficient.

Bring me the affection of a person I genuinely miss,
I'm thirsty for that cozy, sweet kiss.
Tightened in our naked ties of forgiveness,
The burdens and sorrows of the future's bliss.

The sobbing sky has once more sealed my fate,
I yelled for his name while drowning in destruction.
The love I sought was no longer found,
I lay on the empty, sorrowful road.

The Naughty Crow

Atop the ancient poisonous tree,
The winter's mischievous crow is sitting.
Cawing, cawing, cawing,
Calling the herds of the night to the sunlight that burns idiocy.

I called its attention and signaled with a shush,
It smiled and danced up in the stoic tree—I ran in a rush.
Yes, I am very terrified of that awful, awful crow!
While running, I turned my head;
I saw it finish dancing and bowed.

I went to sit in the same place the next day,
The naughty crow landed on the old tree once again.
I'm terrified, that much is true, but I stayed seated.
Once more, it started cawing, beckoning the nighttime herds,
I never shoved it away and listened to his song.

Goosebumps crept into my skin,
Yet something came upon.
The crow ceased its cawing—
Alas! It gave me a second glance while I was still where I was.
The same thing happened yesterday, but I decided not to run.
The crow gasped in surprise, cocked its head,
And uttered a wise counsel.

"Young man, death calls on someone who is less tortured.
The sky's hue is not what it first appears to be.
Fly up to the moon of scrutiny.
You'll find out how to open your heart to the world.
Blossoming flowers of petunias by the rock,
Gardens along the deep ocean.
The shallow mountain's heart is littered with vase fragments.
Taking in the death's sunlight,
Brought by the evening's agony."

Before I could say a word,
The crow departed the aged tree—
Vanished towards the horizon.
The following day,
I'm sitting here on the bench in the wild forest once more,
Awaited the mischievous crow's arrival on the venerable tree—
Alas! Discouraged, I felt.
It was never seen again.
Nevertheless, the sage advice persisted in my head.

I heaved my feet out of the dense forest,
I brought myself home and started to consider those words.
Lonely, yes, I'm lonely—I could not figure out the riddle.
My mind began to grow with something.
And came the answer of tomorrow.

Symphony of the Sundered Hearts

It was in September 1939,
I found myself standing by the line.
Alone, yes, I am—
With ragged, filthy clothes on;
Dry mustard sketched on my cheek.
Hands clutching a frayed, blackish-blue scarf.
Cling on my worn-out green shirt,
A paper with my name, age, destination, and date of birth.

Children in their nice coats;
Papers pinned on their collars,
Their hands clung to the big suitcases.
Parents embracing their dearest ones,
Love and sacrifice were emblazoned on their faces.
Bravery, in their heart drums.

The fart of the train made me realize I was lost,
Onboarding—I have to, and stop by the unfamiliar faces of no one.
Hope in my heart surged up in heaven,
Praying for a hand to warm up my bleak future.

"Child, where are your parents?
Why are your shoes torn with bullets from a thousand stories?"
To my surprise, I did not see,
A beautiful young lady behind was quietly watching me.

The colour of the dying rainbow in my heart,
Once again turned its light up in the sky.
I turned and tucked the smile beneath my chest,
Ready to utter the symphony of my life.

"Your eyes speak a hundred colours of yesterday,
Yet there is no trace of pencil on your lips.
Can you bring me a sketch of your journey, child?
I shall tell your story in a book for people to read."

She cut me off just as the orchestra began to play in my lungs,
I revealed the curve of emotion and politely shook my head.
"Your generosity soared my feet unto great appreciation,
Yet I do not want anyone to know my situation.
My mother and father sealed me under their feet of burdens,
I do not want to borrow another sorrow behind the beautiful curtains."

"You may ask, under whose roof I shall bring my head?
Who will feed me fresh and hot bread?
Who's going to prepare my bed?
Who's going to cover my ears and wrap me out of dread?
You shall not worry about me, gorgeous lady, for I shall be fine.
The morrow will draw me the future of his design."

Words did not slip off her tongue,
A beautiful smile remained on her face.
I moved my feet from the queue,

And moved towards the door of the departing train.
She raised her hand and waved goodbye to me,
In her eyes, seen the beauty and honesty.
The sky of the whimpering future,
Bestowed me luck of the coming destiny.

I sat along with the other children my age in the small cabin,
Witnessing the soft cries of others calling their parents.
I uttered no words on them—
Silence brings great peace and comfort to anyone in burden.
My eyes caught the running barren—
It shed tears of pain,
Away, away, it waved at everyone on the train.
"Goodbye for now, my home; I shall see you soon once again."

Moving forward on this journey,
I woke up when I heard the loud fart of the train again.
Lifting the eyelids off my sight,
A cloudy image of a young girl before me stood.
Her hazel eyes glued into mine—
She took it away before I could.
She quickly ran out of the cabin; others followed,
Clueless and confused, I went to hit the alien road.

"Child, we met again.
What a small world that we have!
May I have your name at least?

For me to remember you for the rest of my life.
The morrow will bestow me another world to live on,
Where I can rest and watch everyone peacefully."

Once again, the feet of ours led us to one another,
The sleeping rainbow woke up for the second time,
Lighting up the dark sorrow beneath my chest.
I find no reason for me to keep her company,
Yet the pulse of destiny pushed my mouth to spill my life.

"My name is Liam Ali Nithercott,
My parents abandoned me by the doorstep of resentment.
I grew up to be someone's slave—alas!
My blood was coloured with wrath.
I have no reason why I should tell you everything about me,
Yet you seemed to be a great lady.
I wish you the best in your life,
May you be peaceful and happy with your remaining time."

I care less about how she'd feel,
Hatred brings me no generosity.
The curse of my parents in me is sealed,
My heart once crashed, but it was fixed with ferocity.
I do not mean to bow with great insolence,
It just happens that she came across with a brazen.

My feet brought me to an old, small house,

A few steps away from where the train dropped me.
I knocked on the door three times,
No one answered.
I tapped my knuckles again on the wooden door,
Yet failed—no one is inside.

"Child, what are you doing?
Are you lost at the moment—Alas!
Let me lend a hand for you, young one."
There was the voice of the young lady again.
She is somewhat of a bother in my life,
I want to get rid of anyone who's not welcome on my journey.

"I bring you peace and forgiveness, gorgeous lady,
Yet you are bothering me.
Could you please bring your feet somewhere else?
Where you could never see me.
I appreciate your kindness,
However, I shall give you piece of rest.
Your wish to help anyone—I am happy to hear!
But I am not in need of anyone's hand.
Bring forth your business on your own,
I shall mind mine all alone."

I knew she was displeased of my words,
Yet a smile remained in her warm presence.
She remained staring at me, as if trying to read the phrases in my eyes,

My face remained before the door.
Then, she raised her hand, holding a big key,
Her eyes filled with tears.

The skies poured shame on my head,
The paint of embarrassment coloured my pale skin.
I brought my head down and apologized—
Swallowing one's pride is that hard.
I folded my knees before her,
Cried until the wounds began to open again—
Wounds of yesterday's swords in my neck.
Slavery taught me to become a tough, shameless child,
Pain and a colourless future, locked in the shackles of defeat.

"Child, how did you stumble before my house?
I do not know anyone will come except for my son.
Who sent you here—please tell me the name.
You might be lost, but I can put the roof on your head as if you are mine."

"Forgive me, for I do not know where I should go.
My parents left me—where are they? I do not know.
I found this address of yours by the window:
Forgive me, for I want to have a home.
I am desperate to find bread to fill my belly.
I wish for a warm arm to bring back my heart's symphony.
A future—I do not know what it means.
All I know is that I live in an empty world."

The gorgeous lady cried more before me,
Her eyes did not speak of agony.
It was filled with happiness and glory,
Which brought me to wonder and inquiry.
"My my, you are the son I have waited for too long.
You are that child I always wish to sing a song.
Your eyes speaks it all,
How you longed for someone's love and care.
Forgive me, my child—it pains me to say—
My eyes did not recognize your stance."

I spelt not a word,
Silence is what she heard.
Bitter taste of fate,
Reached the bottom of my tongue.
Anguish, to which my heart clung,
Wished I never met her, nor did I come,
I forgive no one—no, I'll forget everyone!

My feet began to heave away,
Agony smashed my heart to pieces.
My fingers ran to the paper clipped on my shirt—
I pulled it off hard.
Crystal-liquid rained on my dirty cheeks,
The more I felt weak.

"Your heart whispered in my ear;
I heard it, son.
Don't let hatred eat you fully,
Let me fix the orchestra of our relationship.
Bring your eyes to the colour of the wind on the horizon,
See the beauty of the ocean that once dreamed of reaching you.
Let my hand wipe the tears of pain,
Let me colour your life once again."

"I am only twelve now, Mama,
But I had learned a lot of things about the world:
Once the stars shower the light of wisdom,
They'd glow even in the darkest chamber.
Once the match burns,
It will never come back to its original form.
Beauty is not about how light one's skin is.
But how gorgeous is her or his heart.
Everything in the world is not the same as you thought it was.
Be careful when trusting someone—horns are never seen immediately."

"The symphony of yours might have called my heart to come near you,
Yet I do not wish for my fate to come across someone who brought me sorrow.
You were never there when I needed to stand,
Now you seem happy to see me withhold the colours of the rainbow.
I wished for someone to bring me hot bread with a plate of ecstasy,

But I do not wish that my mother would bring me such,
Alas! 'Mother' puts a sword in my heart—I shall call you not!
You don't deserve anyone—you abandoned me to suffer—
In exchange of papers with amounts of abundance."

With that, my feet continued to heave away with goodbye,
Her eyes were screaming with guilt and forgiveness—
Yet, I did not mind.
I let fury swallow the whole of me,
Blood cursed the word that describes her name—put the blame on her, not me!
The vision of distorted smiles of mine together with someone else shifted away,
That'll never happen—not in my life, ever!

Days passed; I found myself roofless.
I beg for a penny from people who go by; they care less.
Knocking on every door,
Held my hand for a small piece of bread.
Frightened, surprised, screams—
Mostly give me the look of dread.
My belly growls with hunger,
Yet I have nothing to fill it.

Hopeless, I sat down by the fence,
Thinking to myself, how should I commence?
Shadows of my words on the woman began to grow before me,
Hurt—I am; betrayed by my own existence.

"My child, my child, hear the symphony of our sundered hearts,
Bring the music of the rivers calling you beneath.
Let the path be fixed with the embrace of kindness,
Bring forth your cold hands into the fire of love."

The world hoisted when the soothing voice of a woman entered my ear,
Lethargic, I raised my head at the vague image of someone before me.
The rainbow beneath flickered with joy,
That feeling, I knew who it was—Mother,
The woman whom I cursed for the rest of my life.

Pride etched in my chest,
Yet my tongue slept on the sealed, pale, and dry mouth.
My trembling hands crawled gradually,
Begging for hot bread to fill my dying belly.
"P-Please… a hot... bread,"
I barely could open my mouth—woe! Blame me!

"Shush, my child, I shall bring you home.
In my arms, you'll never live again in doom.
Allow me to make up for the mistakes I have done.
Let me show you the love that was long gone."
"Forgive, for I was scared of the scars that may bring me shame.
I left you in exchange for a fiver and a tenner.
I hear no reason for me to leave you behind,

But the voyager life that crossed the lightning of uncertainty pulled the fear in me."

Her words echoed until now, when my hair had turned gray,
As my pen curves every letter on this poem, her whispers call in my ears.
Tears of loneliness and anguish, I once shared with her,
The longing to replace it with a joyful symphony knocks at my heart.
Regrets eat me every single day,
But the caress of forgiveness brings hope to the skies.
The silhouette of destiny between the sundered hearts,
Will become the portrait of true love and hatred.

Tagay, Waraynun: Beckon of Camaraderie

"Tagay, doy; Tagay, day!"
"Tagay, Lo; Tagay, nay!"
A glass full of red wine embraced by a hand,
Beckon of unity—it's what it stands.
A single gulp is equivalent to million happiness,
Curve of appreciation shown in every lips.

Tuba is what its name,
The pride of Waraynun; it remained the same.
Every fiesta, every occasion,
Never will be missed on the tables of Leyteños and Samarnons.
"Bahal nga Tuba" —what drinkers mostly seek,
Lurkes in their throat the taste of bitterness,
yet delicious and sweet.

Unique pride of the Waraynuns,
Brings everyone together.
"Bahal nga Tuba" on the table,
Tightens people closer.
A cling of glass with red wine bubbling,
Creates the music of harmony—in every heart sings.

Goodnight Kiss in the Lionheart Street

Fleecy clouds carried me up to the seventh heaven,
Butterflies fluttered in my stomach,
Upon the thought of you reached the inner of my heart.
Sat before the gorgeous vanity,
Brush, slide, curve, and blush, I went.
Saw a beautiful woman after a while,
I smiled once again, thinking this'd be a special night.

Dropping the tight robe unto the floor,
The elegant fit-and-flare dress embraced me.
I slid my feet unto the white 2-inched heeled sandals,
And toward the door, I walked straight.

We met on Lionheart Street,
You took my hand to your old, yet sweet, car.
You pulled something from the back of it,
And before me appeared a romantic bouquet of anemones.
Tears filled my eyes with happiness,
You wiped it with a gentle kiss.

We drove to the nearest café,
Shared a piece of vanilla cake, drooling a bittersweet chocolate.
The taste of one bite is somewhat different—
I love it.

Your smile soughed the aura of twilight,
Blooms in my heart, your name—forever.
Every sketch of our touch,
Felt like a thousand fireworks dancing in the starlight.

Nine o'clock in the evening,
You took my hand out of the café.
You brought me to your car,
We drove to another place to enjoy the moment of ours.

We sat down by the long bridge,
Watched the stars waving at us.
We talked, we laughed, we made jokes,
Until silence sealed our mouths.
Then all of a sudden, a voice freed my lips,
When you asked me something I least expected—
"Will you be my girlfriend?"

I was unable to answer your question,
It was quite surprising, I admit it.
I don't know what happened next,
All I remember was a warm, soft, gentle lips—
We kissed!

After the splendid night,
You drove me back to Lionheart Street.

Your lips landed on my forehead,
Whispered the sweetest goodnight kiss.
My hand wrapped yours to mine—as if it didn't want you to go,
Which I hoped I did.
Tears filled up my eyes—I have no idea why.
"I love you," I heard it.
My mouth was sealed, unable to speak the words—
Everything is just overwhelming.
You asked me to let you go,
And until now, I regret doing so.

You walked to your car,
And the last thing I saw was your smile before a deafening sound came upon us.
My eyes opened; you were never there.
Then someone whispered in my ears—
You gladly said goodbye,
Because we'll never see each other again.
Not for now, not tomorrow,
But we'll meet again in heaven.

Melancholy

Light starts to fade away,
Came the cold embrace once again.
Beat of hopes,
Softened into silent weep.
Smooth waves of the melody inside,
Gone wild in despair.

Insanity called my soul—
He's a friend of mine under the dark clouds and lightning.
Strength left my heart,
Dead hopes surged in me.

Song of the Blues

Up in the mountain's peak cries a canorous violin,
Hoping to be heard by the lang syne's love.
Echoes in every note the purity and joy,
Commanding the wind to call for the lost promises.

Reminiscence of touch of the future's breathe,
Dance in one's thought—the blues.
Birds came along,
Sang the beautiful song of colorless libretto.
May lang syne's ear catch the whisper of the one who summons.

The tip of every words,
Eyes cry of betrayal.
Behold—the heart's desire beams melancholia.
Alas! Thirsty hands beg for leniency—
Innocence knocks on the doors for the truth.

The song of blues should be heard,
Not by thousand ears, but one.
To the sound of the never-ending call of violin,
May mercy rain down its parched hopes.

Lullaby of One's Freedom

Silhouettes of chains,
Appeared up in the gorgeous sunset.
Sick and wounded hands cried—
Begged for help, yet no one heard her howls.

The lang syne roared—
Guilt awoke, Alas!
"Crystal moonlight broke wonders and misery,
Beckoned by the hues of presage; behind the curtains,
Awaits the whisper of vociferation."
He, who tied the white soul spoke,
His tongue preaching deadly words;
People grasped for his cold sweat—sheer absurdity!
The chiseler's blood sucked their veins.

Behold, the keys of fetters that fastened the feet and hands,
Bows before deception.
Cheered with evil eyes stuck on the walls,
Champagnes of great subterfuge—how egocentric!
Bless the eyes who saw the truth,
Hold in them the shackles of his defeat.

Upon the day of execution took place,
The innocent soul was escorted to the gallows—
Woe! Shows in her eyes the colorless story.

"Some pulchritudinous maiden hides a scar,
Not seen in the face—it's in the derrière.
Do not be tempted by the thousand layers of maquillage!
No matter how thick it is,
One's secret would not be able to hide."
Her voice spilled silence among the crowd;
They were hypnotized of her angelic lullaby.

Then, resonated a response from nowhere,
"Voiceless screams inside the bar of shame,
Hands gripped on the brick of hell—
May she be heard;
She is the Mother's crystal heart.
Look beneath the throat of that celestial being,
A venom sleeps;
Awakes on the fourth, will sip on one's tongue to deceive."

He, who speaks faceless,
Stole one's hood to hide his eyes—
Vanished without a word.
They, who sipped the venom,
Was brought to the world of truth.
They praised and fight for egalitarianism,
Until her hands were freed from the fetters of unfair discernment.

Chimeric tomorrow

Darnes in my little palm,
the sunrise in the east.
Thread and needles playfully brighten tomorrow,
Effervescence etches on visages—Hourrah!

"Mama" and "Dada" —
Saccharine sound of innocence brings comfort to uneasiness.
Hourglass of dawn, please bring down the sand;
Call of patience—I missed it.

Orchestra of kiss refracts in my little house;
Neonatal love sings in my tiny heart.
Mini feet of mine wiggle—
You feel it!
Mellow touch creeps into delicate hands,
The taste of one's white nurture is sweetfully admiring.

One day, a rainbow will come after a hurricane,
Little feet would walk and run in a ravine.
Together with the pillar of home during the winter night,
Stars of horizon bestowed the fragile bonds.

Sunrise mended on my little palm—Formocity!
Yet, a berceuse of melancholia heaves from my lungs,

Spring ran away; disappeared into the million miles of grief.
The little angel with chimeric tomorrow is me—
Bygone's unborn optimist.

Art of Society

Freedom of speech—once mouth's death,
Justice—serve for those who can breathe.
Smooth hands on poverty—wait! Say 'cheese'!
Straight roads ahead—hold on, where is the plate of salmon?

Clic-cloc-clic-clic,
Went on the box with alphabets.
Bravery shapes behind the formed words.
Bullets of every phrase,
Encouraged the rope to end a life.

'Personality' equivalent to 'what a person wears',
'Looks' should be accurate to his or her 'career'.
'Respect'—do you hold a degree?
'Equality'—do you own a business, two or three?

Curse hides beneath the lines of judgement,
Pages of the truth are closed.
Behind every art,
Curls the sad reality that the modern generation has.

Impostor

Darling of orchid leaf kissed the soft perseverance,
Sway down the bottom of armoured affection
—a cactus plant.
Wires of questions knitted on one's thumb,
Bark of ignorance hit the theories—cry!

Poison—the healer of retarded feelings,
Satisfaction hurrays in every swallow.
Swim up in the skies of sharks—
Behold, the teeth of knives shaped into hearts.
Be mindful of what you see;
Some impostor hides in every shell.

Art of Words

Freedom. Color. Time.
Hardwork. Spring. Water.
Fortitude. Alliance. Diligence. Honesty.
Amalgamation. Ecstasy. Hollow.
Despair. Disease. Torment. Assuage. Red. Time.

White lies. Symphonized falsity. Broken figures.
Poisonous promises. Vocalized blade. Painted scarcity.
Humorous cries. Bitter marriage. Doomed happiness.
Counterclockwise encounter. Faked intelligence. Lost power.

Running towards one's dream.
Pushing the fire of demur.
Breathing roses; growing aspiration.
Smiles behind the bars of freedomless.
Clap on the chest of persistence.
Shout with tears of success.
Sweat of determination.
The one who wins the trophy,
Are the people who never give up.

Withered Love

Chicory danced in the middle of the plain field,
A little girl picked it up; kissed it petals—
The gorgeous chicory blushed.
Fell in love with her oceanic eyes,
The weed blossomed in joy.

Laid on her smooth hand—
Ah, it's heaven!
Chicory smiled,
In her hand she does not want to ever go.
Kiss there, kiss here, kiss everywhere—
Happiness locked their knots together.

Years and years passed,
Chicory stayed with the little girl—now a woman!
She began to cut the thread between them,
Chicory was hurt—yet smile she went.

One night, the woman came home,
A guy's hand was imprinted on her wrist—
The little chicory was torn.
Once again, the woman cut their thread—
Little by little, it's breaking.
Chicory knew it's painful,
Yet she left for a good reason.

Azaleas

Her charm sprangles;
The world is at peace with her beauty.
Her gorgeous eyes twinkles,
The nuance caress pulls euphony.

Light color of her skin,
Wakes curiosity—what makes her like it?
Such a pleasant to the eyes of many,
Her soft whispers are lullabies of good fortune.

Yet, do not be fooled by her beauty,
Her name is Azaleas,
The pulchritudinous scourge—woe!
Stay away from her if you wish to breathe more.

Morning Soul

Sun wakes up;
Painted the skies with its yellow and red colors.
The plants opened their eyes,
Shook their hairs to bring such a harmonious silent scream.
The birds on their nests,
Began stretching;
Their throat itch with the orchestra of music—
Pleasant to the ears!
The wind finally came to visit,
Kissing everyone with its fresh and gentle blow.

"Good morning," greets the crow with its long trumpet,
"It's time for your responsibility, man—feed me!"
Calls the cow from a little far, mooing to heaven.
Soft and gentle grass tickles the pots—
"May the kind man let me lay alone.
I bring no harm, yet my love grows within the garden."

Music to the ears,
The orchestra of the birds.
Whisper of the wind,
Gentle touch on the surrounding.
Dancing trees,
Enjoying the caress of the morning soul.

Butterfly of Her Promise

Twilight kissed our eyes in Ohayo,
Hands tied together with the knot of our vigilant love.
Tongue lurked for sagacity;
Chests pampered innocence of one's feelings.

Your voice under the stars,
Your cozy laughter with my jokes.
Smell of your blackish blond hair,
Brings a line on my lips—I'm inlove.

"One day, you'll stand by an altar,
A butterfly will come and kiss your forehead.
Do not break its wings,
For it is the kiss of farewell and passion."
Your eyes speak it all—
The bloom of an unsought flower.

Colors in my head,
The clouds of fear and uncertainty.
Yet my love grew harder in my heart,
Until a plant turned into a tree—strong and brave.
I walked on dragons, crossed fated death,
Swum on the fire of perserverance,
Until the plant made its way to become a strong tree—
it's my love for you.

Footprints of wilting flowers lingered on every road,
I care less; we shall carry on.
Little did I know,
Every piece of your hair brought it to life to bloom again.

The night before you departed away,
Into somewhere I cannot go,
You hold my hand tightly,
And whispered the sweet melody of your promise—
The butterfly on my forehead.

Standing on the altar,
Beside you lying with your eyes closed.
A gorgeous butterfly kissed my forehead—
It broke me, indeed.
Because I know it was you who kissed goodbye.

Desire

What's from the distant past causes me to regret the present?
What gaps exist inside that nobody else has seen?
Which of the two roads should I take?
Taking into account the positive effects?

If I feel out of touch with reality,
How will I know I'm on the right track?
Going far down into the pitch-black void,
What is waiting for me on the ground that weighs me down?

The deeper I delve,
The more I regret it.
The box of sorrow is illuminated with hope.
But why do I still feel so gloomy and depressed?
Supposedly, tomorrow when morning comes,
the sun will rise in the sky.
Oh, I hope it will rain to fill this dry life of mine.
Pour me into a pretty vessel.
Every moment I wake up, I want tranquility.

Your Name

Your name is something I still treasure;
It's something I wanted to keep forever.
Your name is the only one I want to call out;
I can do it, unfortunately, in a voiceless shout.
Whenever I miss you,
I want to smolder away like a depressed candle.
I couldn't help but look for you from every angle.
Ideally, I'd forget your name,
However, it's simply too impossible.

However, I believe one day,
I'll never think about you again in my heart.
Someday, your name will just melt and depart.
Your name will fade into obscurity.
It will simply vanish and disappear easily.

Despair

I hold a lovely soul in my grasp,
Whirling in time to the melody's beat.
She's wailing inside,
But shows no face of sympathy.

You're worn out, poor soul.
In the bed of thorns of the future, sleep.
It will undoubtedly bring you peace.
Nevertheless, it hurts and is bloody.

Word of Advice

Suicide—oh, what a big word!
A word that everyone murmurs in anguish,
Without considering what this really entails.
Oh, you wretched soul, have you ever had self-doubts?

How will it be up there when you pass away?
Would you like to feel yourself in the sky?
Will your tears of hopelessness dry?
Close your eyes and reflect for a time.
What is death, and what is life?

Have you ever witnessed the light of freedom?
If you didn't look for it, you wouldn't find it.
They claim that suicide is a free choice.
Poor soul, don't let your thoughts deceive you!

Have yourself some faith,
And by fire, avoid being caught!
Don't heed to the voices of death;
Instead, feel your heart.
If you choose life,
You will understand what breathing is.

Painless Color

The hopeful thread is severed by a painful scissor,
And it gracefully let itself fall.
The throng was drawn in by its soulless, silent movement.
Surprisingly, a dubious mindset began to emerge.
However, it does nothing but remain still.
Nothing but calm was sensed by the cut thread,
Because it treats suffering as if it were merely another toy in life.

It simply kept gazing the sky,
Like nothing just transpired.
Soon, silver liquid began to flow down its lovely, dejected face.
It then shut its eyes, seeing nothing but peace.

Fighters of the Forest

Along the tranquil mountain's stream,
A lonely melody may be heard.
A lovely grin can be shattered
by the sobbing eagle's singing above the tree.
In the downpour, combatants dash across the forest,
Found themselves disoriented in the dead of night.
From above, the stars radiated dispassionate light.
Nowhere did they find any hope.

Dead trees remained in place, motionless.
Awaiting the life that tomorrow will bring.
They had seen the sweet lovebirds fly away.
Leaving behind scars from the past and a bleak future.
The forests, which once played a lovely melody of life
Becomes now the dread of hope for hazy tomorrows.

Fear Within

I'd rather keep myself in my shell;
Rejection terrifies me.
I want to shout my name in victory—no, I cannot!
The judgment and curiosity in their eyes is palpable.
It bothers me—I kept it inside.
Must I venture outside?
Would it be better for me to remain silent?

Tell me, tell me!
Oh, tell me, dear answerer!
What must I do?
Am I supposed to keep this forever?
Alas! It's not a victory,
Just some lies, I suppose.
It has to do with that emotion,
the one that endures forever.

Shadow of Reality

The eagle came flying toward me,
which I witnessed.
Its eyes display both rage and sympathy.
Run, run away, myself!
Hide your hideous emotions!
I'm in such a panic now—no, it's too late, dear.

The claws had snagged me.
It whisked me away—away from myself.
Ah, what a strange place this is;
I should yell for help!

I shouted at the top of my lungs,
hoping someone would hear.
But it was powerless; everyone simply vanished.
I suddenly saw a flurry of memories.
I recognized myself in it while I was present with everyone.

My attempts to blend in have gone unnoticed.
With friends and actual family,
everyone is busy.
My heart was literally tearing into bits.
Fortunately, I received consolation from someone.

And she goes by the name of Loneliness.

She has a certain way of being friendly to me.
She drags me back to her sad past,
when everything is unpleasant.
We both lead the same existence, which is useless and dead.
So, we both made the decision to cut our lives short with a knife.

Forgive for Freedom

A soothing voice of pardon,
Quietly whispered in my ears.
I shut my eyes,
Felt the heart's tender and loving embrace.
It's okay to grieve and release your guilt;
everything will turn out just fine.

My eyes opened, and they were filled
with a brightness of emancipation.
How amazing it feels on the inside;
how fortunate to be alive!
I feel my chest tighten with joy.
Undoubtedly, it is the greatest.

Farewell Letter

The brisk wind mumbled,
A dejected grin emerged.
The astringent liquor was sipped,
My lips were lured in by sweetness.
the whiff of yesterday's promise,
All that is left now are memories.
The injuries had healed,
Scars did still exist.

The journey that we shared,
There were no longer any footprints.
Oh, the lovely lullaby, now sung through tears.
One's love is being embraced by you.
Forgotten how sweet mine is.
Your tender, delicate touch on my heart,
Are now the stabs of the enemy.

I most likely made a mistake,
You escaped my grasp.
I'd never want to part with you.
However, you're too big and strong.
Someone else is calling you now love.
Oh, what a charming name!
Wish I could still call you the same
But it's certain that it won't happen again.

Wish of the Hopeless Heart

I'm scared of every dancing lettuce,
Wildly blooming across the bridge of fate.
I want to cross with someone's hand holding mine,
Yet as I reached the other,
Realization hit me—not a single one exist.
No matter how I try to call someone's name,
No one dares to hear me.

I cry because I'm in pain,
I cry because I'm weak.
I cry because I'm too scared.
I cry because I'm falling down unto darkness.

The questions lurks in every cell of my body,
Do I deserve to die?
Do I deserve to disappear?
Why is the color of the rose's petals
Turned into a darkish alley—for my soul.

I want someone to hear my scream,
Please let me bow on tomorrow's kiss.
I'm alone, yet I fight—but to whom should I?

I feel numb from morning 'til dawn,
I care less about everything—I'm numb—I'm dumb.

Bring me the cookie of the sweet desires,
Hate to see mourns of fueled in sympathy.
Talking to a bitter grass,
Caressed my lonely heart.

No one will ever understand what I'm trying to say,
But I don't mind.
Thank you for spending time on this.
May you have good lives.

Do You Remember You?

Do you remember you?
Crawling with your hands on knees on the floor.
Your toothless smile,
Facing your 'mama' and 'dada' from afar.

Do you remember you?
The sweet giggles from tickles,
The sweet cries every night,
Whenever you ask your milk in a bottle.

Do you remember you?
Forming the letters on your mouth,
You play with it until there's no doubt.
Your first word crawling out of your throat,
Became a melodious symphony—
Your parents could not unheard.

Do you remember you?
The progress you had made so far.
From asking your parents' guidance,
Down to doing things little by little on your own.

Years and years go by,
Saw yourself in another home—school.
Nervous at your first,

But you found your best later on.
You stayed for decades,
Until you wore the hat of success.

What have you learned so far, my friend?
From the tears that rained your cheeks,
Cries of uncertainties,
Down to the meadows of sadness,
That you could not express.

What have you learned so far, my friend?
Letting other people come and go,
Asking them to hold on for a while—
But they insisted to walk away.

What have you learned so far, my friend?
With every clings of champagne,
Every clic-clocs of keyboards,
And shaking your hands with others.
Life is full of surprises, they say—
You don't know what's ahead.
Bracketing yourself with ventures of self-confidence
Will bring forward a good morrow.
Might seem a bit erroneous, I could tell.

Don't ask why, my friend.
Even yourself know the answers about it.
Don't you think it's a bit odd?
To remember yourself being you?

Hopelessly Hoping Ocean

The waves of sadness runs to the shore.
The tears of loneliness swim on the ocean floor.
Keep me distance from your heart,
I will continue to be torn apart.

The cold breeze of hope runs in my veins,
The love I felt before for you still remains.
Yes, I'm hopelessly hoping ocean you had forgotten,
Yet your name, our memories in my heart will never be unwritten.

Strong

Lived in life with thorns of pain,
Screamin' out—hoping someone would hear.
Tried to find a way out of the darkness,
Yet failed, failed, and failed again.

Searched for the voices who said,
"Will never leave you behind until the end."
But couldn't recognize them anymore—
Everyone's mouth are sealed with silence.

Heard the clap of reality,
Awaken me out of fantasy.
No one is there to help except myself—
I agree.
No matter how lost I may be,
I will stand on my own.
No matter how strong the win is,
I will never be blown.

Painfully Sweet Illusions

You came closer,
Whispered to my ear.
Said the words,
Promised you'll never disappear.
Sweet words of yours,
Made me smile.
Only to find out,
Those were just moments for a while.

Kept you inside my head,
Thought that you are here.
But reality slapped me,
Made me realize you aren't real.
My heart crashed down,
Hoping you would heal it.
However, how can it be possible,
If you don't even exist?

Thread of Life

Scissor of pain cuts the hoping thread,
Yet it painlessly let itself fall.
Its silent emotionless motion,
Caught the attention of the crowd.
Surprised, questionable mindset started to grow,
Yet it laid there still.

The threat felt nothing but peace,
For it thought pain is just another toy in one's life.
It just stared up in the sky,
As if nothing has happened just now.
Later, silver liquid rilled down its beautiful sad face.
Then, it closed its eyes—
Nothing more seen but peace.

Echoes of Lost Hope

Melody of loneliness flows down the stream of the peaceful mountain,
Music of the weeping eagle above the tree,
Could break the sweet smile.
Fighters in the rain run through the woods—
Found themselves lost in the middle of the night.
Stars from above showed emotionless light,
They found no hope anywhere around.

Dead trees stood still in their places,
Waiting for tomorrow to pour them life.
Sweet birds of love had flown away from them—
Leaving hopeless future with the scars of yesterday.
The woods, which was once a beautiful music of life,
Becomes now the fear of hope for tomorrow's blurry visions.

Lost in the Whispers

The cold wind whispered,
A sad smile appeared.
The bitter liquor was sipped,
Sweetness lured unto my lips.
The scent of yesterday's promise,
Now fading into memories.

Wounds had been healed,
Scars did remain.
The path we crossed together,
Footprints had disappeared.
Oh, my sweet lullaby,
Now singing with tears in her eyes.

You are embracing someone's love,
Forgotten how sweet was mine.
Your gentle and fragile touch in my heart,
Now has became an enemy's stabs.

It probably was my mistake—
You slipped out of my hand.
Never want to let you go,
But you're too strong and heavy.

Now somebody else calls you 'love'—
    Oh, what a sweet name!
I wish I still could call you the same,
Yet surely, it will never happen again.

Resonation of Absences

The call of dawn passed by—
Heard no voices of your heart.
My footprints on the sand waited for yours to join,
But waves had erased it—faded.

Tears of loneliness flowed,
Still waited for you to wipe it.
You never did—you never came,
A bitter smile of mine broke my heart into pieces.

The Light Within

Soothing voice of forgiveness,
Whispered gently in my ears.
I closed my eyes,
Felt the warm and sweet embrace of heart.
It's okay to cry and let out the guilt—
Things will work out just fine.

My eyes opened,
Light of freedom came to me.
How beautiful it does feel inside,
How grateful it is to live.
Happiness drawn to my chest—
It is the best, indeed.

I Understand What I don't Understand

Ill-mended thoughts crossed my head—Alas, I'm scared.
What am I scared of?—I don't know
Clouded ferocity of yesterday's keep barging the closed door,
I'm getting insane—put the blade down the unscarred skin.

Help, I want it—but how do I shout when my voice has deepen down the shallow bottom.
Pain, it is inside—but I don't see it;
I don't feel anything at all.
My eyes are dry to feather down the fall of tears,
Am I insane—yes I am I could say.

I wrote a note before,
Asking myself to be strong.
But where is it right now?
I don't understand myself…
I really don't.

Couldn't find any words to tickle down the clear sheet,
Where could I possibly get the words.
Shower the colorless soul—pray.
Don't let it die in the midst of emptiness.

About the Author

Nery Joy Ochea

Nery Joy Ochea, a writer from Leyte, Philippines, embarked on her writing journey at the age of nine and persevered until the age of 22. Her first inspiration was Joanne Kathleen Rowling, after she finished reading the compilation of Harry Potter books at an early age. This was followed by William Shakespeare and John Ronald Reuel Tolkien. In January 2023, she achieved her long-awaited dream of becoming a published author with Ukiyoto Publishing House, a publishing house located in Canada. Alongside this accomplishment, her exceptional works were recognized by a literary magazine in the Philippines.

Before her success as a published author, she gained valuable experiences working in call center companies in Cebu. The experience of communicating with people from different cultures molded her ability to understand life and people, which in turn helped shape her writing. Soon after, she was invited as a guest speaker in an international school in Luzon, where she had the chance to inspire young individuals in their aspirations to become authors in the future, even if it was done virtually.

Currently, she is a dedicated Bachelor of Arts in Communication student at Biliran Province State University in Naval, Biliran. Though it was not her initial choice to be part of the School of Arts and Sciences, she has fallen in love with the program and has deepened her connections with everyone she has met. She believes that she is meant to be in this program due to her abilities and skills in expressing emotions through writing and communication.

Despite experiencing rejections from various publishing houses in the United States, Europe, and the Philippines, Nery Joy did not let herself become demotivated. Instead, she continued to fuel her words, knowing that one day she would be able to ignite the fire of inspiration in others.

www.ingramcontent.com/pod-product-compliance
Lightning Source LLC
LaVergne TN
LVHW041541070526
838199LV00046B/1780